Hello!

Julie Ellis

OXFORD
UNIVERSITY PRESS

Contents

Talk

There are lots of ways to say hello.
When I see my dad, I talk to him.

On the phone

Hello!

Sometimes I phone my friend,

or he phones me.

Text messages

I want to say hello to my aunty.
Mum helps me to send her a text message.

She sends me a message too.

Email

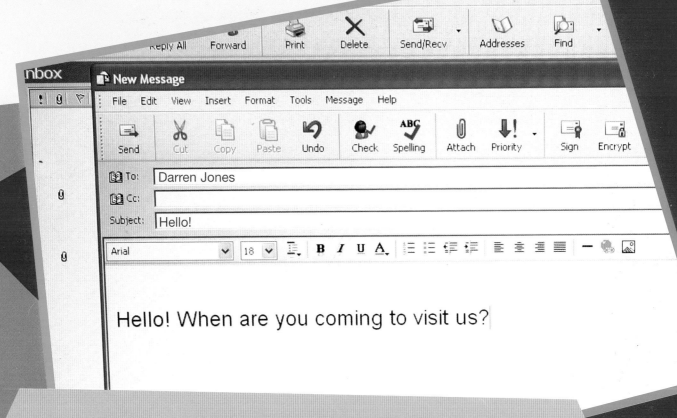

I send an email to my cousin in America.

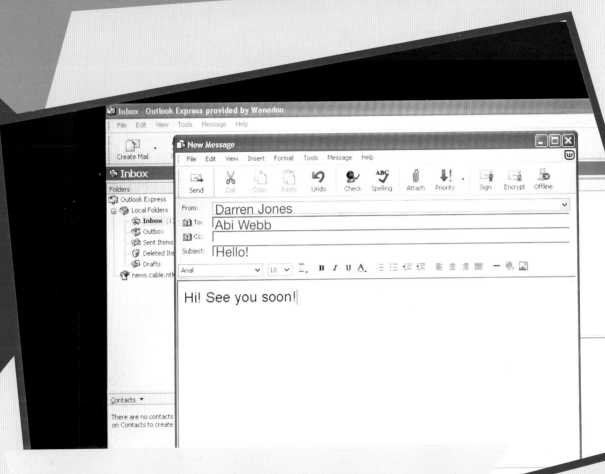

He sends an email back to me.

Letters

Grandad writes me a letter.

I write back to him.

Signing

My brother is deaf. He signs to me to say hello.

I sign back to my brother.

Goodbye!

Goodbye

I wave to my mum to say goodbye.

Goodbye

She waves back to me.

15

Index

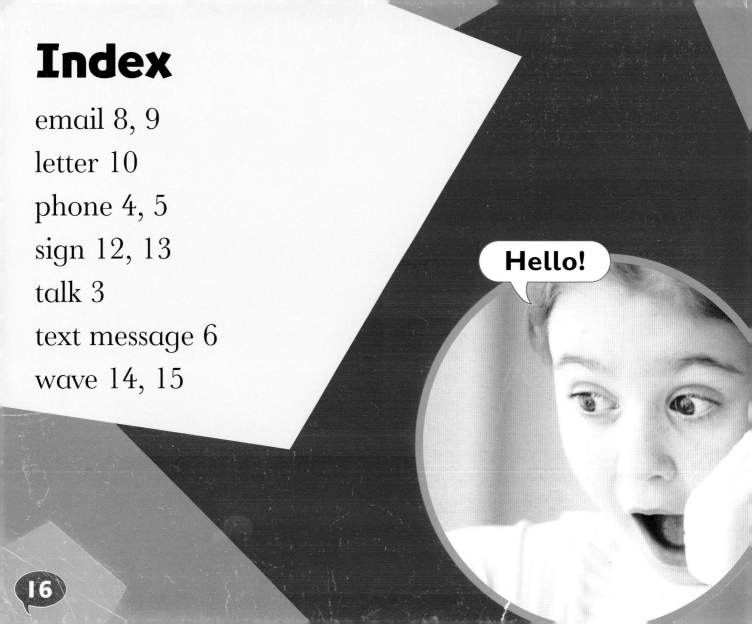